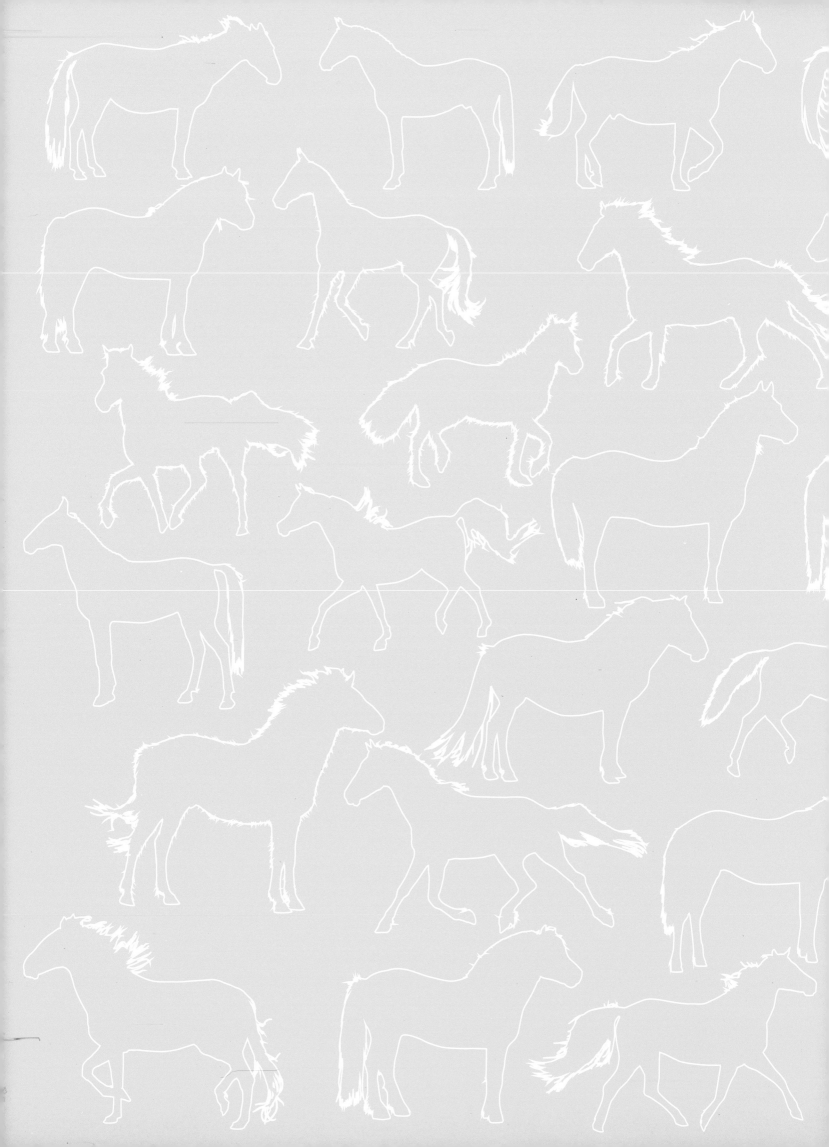

THE
MAGNIFICENT
BOOK
OF
HORSES

THE MAGNIFICENT

❖ BOOK ❖

OF

HORSES

ILLUSTRATED BY
Simon Mendez &
Val Walerczuk

WRITTEN BY
Tom Jackson &
Diana Ferguson

Published by Weldon Owen Children's Books
An imprint of Weldon Owen International, L.P.
A subsidiary of Insight International, L.P.
PO Box 3088
San Rafael, CA 94912
www.insighteditions.com

Weldon Owen Children's Books:
Publisher: Sue Grabham
Creative Director: Bryn Walls
Artists: Simon Mendez and Val Walerczuk
Senior Designer: Tom Forge
Senior Editor: Diana Craig
Editorial Coordinator: Pandita Geary
Consultant: Kim Bryan

Insight Editions:
Publisher: Raoul Goff

ISBN: 978-1-68188-769-2

Manufactured, printed, and assembled in Turkey.
Second printing, October 2021, Levent. LVT1021.
23 22 21 2 3 4 5

Introduction

Horses are found all over the world, peacefully grazing in fields, speeding along racecourses, trotting down city streets, or running wild across plains and marshlands. For centuries, humans have depended on horses to be their helpers and companions. The ancestors of these amazing animals once roamed free in the Earth's wild places, but people caught and tamed them to create all the different breeds we see today.

The Magnificent Book of Horses introduces you to some of the world's most incredible breeds. Meet the powerful Percheron and the mighty Shire. Ride into battle on a Jutland, gallop through wetlands on a Camargue, or round up cattle on the back of a Mustang. Marvel at the dancing Lipizzaners, and discover why Bedouins keep Arab horses in their tents overnight. Learn, too, how Akhal-Teke horses survive freezing nights and scorching days on the steppes of Central Asia.

Get to know some other amazing breeds as well, such as the blue-eyed Icelandic Pony and the little Falabella from Argentina, which is no bigger than a large dog.

Climb into your saddle, take the reins, and ride out into the world with all these fascinating and magnificent horses.

Fact file

There are some special terms used to describe horses, which you'll see in the fact files in this book:

Group: Breeds are divided into Heavy, Light, and Pony groups

Height: Horses are measured in hands. One hand equals 10.16 centimeters (4 inches).

Colors: A horse can be black, brown, spotted, or:
- *Bay* Brown, black mane and tail
- *Chestnut* Reddish-brown
- *Dun* Gold, black mane and tail
- *Gray* Almost white to dark gray
- *Palomino* Creamy gold, white mane and tail

Contents

Camargue

Camargue horses are called the "horses of the sea." They live in the Camargue marshes, where the river Rhône joins the sea in the South of France.

Horses have lived in the Camargue wetlands for 15,000 years. Today's breed is a cross between these ancient animals and Spanish, North African, and other breeds.

In swampy ground, it's hard for horses to trot. The Camargue horse walks or canters through the marshes instead. Camargue horses run wild in small herds called *manades*. Their foals are born in the open.

French cowboys called *gardians* ride these tough little horses. They use them to round up the black Camargue bulls that graze in the marshes.

The Camargue horse feeds on coarse reeds, dry grass, and a plant called samphire that grows in the marshes. Other horses would not like this food.

Fact file

Group: Light horse

Height: 13.1–14.3 hands
  (53–59 in; 135–150 cm)

Color: Gray

Character: Good-natured

Comes from: Rhône delta, France

Used for: Riding

Akhal-Teke

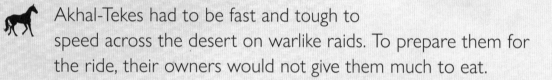

 The Akhal-Teke horse is about 3,000 years old. It is thought to be descended from the ancient wild horses of Central Asia.

 The first Akhal-Teke horses were bred in Turkmenistan in Central Asia. The breed is named after the Teke nomads who lived near the Akhal oasis.

 Akhal-Tekes had to be fast and tough to speed across the desert on warlike raids. To prepare them for the ride, their owners would not give them much to eat.

🐎 To keep them warm at night, Akhal-Teke horses were wrapped in several cozy layers of felt. Nighttime temperatures on the steppes where they lived can drop below freezing.

Fact file

Group: Light horse

Height: 14.3–16 hands
    (59–64 in; 150–163 cm)

Color: Dun, gray, bay, black, with a
    silky sheen

Character: Easygoing

Comes from: Turkmenistan

Used for: Riding

The Akhal-Teke's short coat helps it to stay cool by day in the hot desert region it comes from.

 The fine hairs on the Akhal-Teke's coat give it a shimmering, metallic sheen. This is probably why it has been nicknamed "the Golden Horse."

 In 1935, a group of riders tested the breed's strength. They rode Akhal-Tekes thousands of miles from Turkmenistan to Russia. The journey took 84 days, including three days crossing the barren Karakum Desert.

Holsteiner

- The Holsteiner is one of the oldest breeds of medium-size horse in Germany.

- The breed takes its name from Holstein, an area near the sea in the far north of Germany.

- The first Holsteiners were bred by monks. These men developed the new breed from the small, wild horses that grazed on the windy marshes around their monastery in Holstein.

- Holsteiners were popular with royalty. King Philip II bought Holsteiner stallions for his stud, or breeding, farm in southern Spain. The king ruled a mighty Spanish empire around four hundred years ago.

Fact file

Group: Light horse

Height: 16–17 hands
(64–68 in; 162–173 cm)

Color: Brown, black, bay, gray

Character: Quiet, easygoing

Comes from: Germany

Used for: Riding, sports, pulling carriages

For hundreds of years, Holsteiners were popular coach horses. They worked in teams to pull coaches and carriages.

Early Holsteiners were liked by German farmers because they were strong and reliable workhorses. Soldiers valued them too because they showed courage on the battlefield.

Holsteiners are good in sporting competitions. They canter in a smooth, even way, which makes them comfortable to ride. Their powerful legs and slim bodies make these horses excellent how jumpers.

Connemara

 This is the only pony breed from Ireland. It is named after a region in the west of Ireland, on the wild Atlantic coast.

 Around 1,000 years ago, Viking raiders attacked Ireland. Connemara ponies are thought to be descended from the horses that came with the Vikings in their longships.

 This strong, sturdy pony is perfectly suited to its rugged home. Connemara is a wilderness of mountains, moors, bogs, and marshes.

The Connemara pony always has a small, delicate head, similar to the Arab horse. The two breeds may be related.

Fact file

Group: Pony

Height: 12.2–14.2 hands
(50–58 in; 127–147 cm)

Color: Mostly gray, black, bay, brown, dun

Character: Friendly

Comes from: Ireland

Used for: Riding, pulling loads

Less than a hundred years ago, Irish farmers relied completely on their Connemaras. The ponies pulled plows and carried turf for fires and seaweed to fertilize the fields.

The first Connemara pony was called Cannon Ball. He was used for racing and was famous for his speed and strength. When Cannon Ball died, people came from miles around to say goodbye to him.

Przewalski's Horse

 Herds of these stocky, muscular little horses once roamed free on the wide steppes, or grasslands, between Mongolia and China.

 Until about 140 years ago, people believed that this wild horse had died out. Then a Russian explorer called Nikolai Przewalski found a herd in the remote mountains of Mongolia.

 The Przewalski is also called the Asian Wild Horse or Takhi. It is the only horse that has never been tamed.

 To save the species, scientists have bred captive Przewalskis and released them into the wild. All the Przewalski's Horses alive today are descended from just twelve individuals.

Fact file

Group: Wild

Height: Up to 14 hands (56 in; 142 cm)

Color: Light brown with darker mane, tail and lower legs

Character: Not known

Comes from: Central Asia

Used for: Lives wild

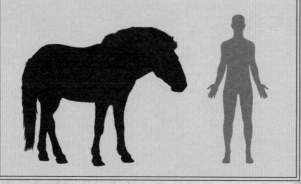

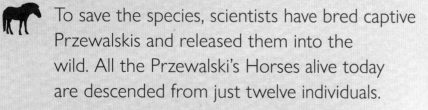

The Przewalski belongs to the same family of horses as zebras and the wild ass. Like them, it has a short, spiky mane. Faint stripes can sometimes be seen on its sides.

In winter, temperatures on the steppes where the Przewalski lives drop well below freezing. The horse grows an extra-thick coat to protect itself from the cold.

Mustang

Mustangs gallop freely across the wide-open spaces of the western United States. They are feral horses, which means that their ancestors were tame but escaped into the wild.

The first Mustangs are thought to be the offspring of horses belonging to the Spanish conquistadors, or conquerors, who arrived in America around 500 years ago.

Mustangs get their name from *mesteño* (pronounced "mess-ten-yo"), a Spanish word that means "wild" or "stray".

The Choctaw and Chickasaw peoples, from the southeastern United States, captured Mustangs from the wild. They used them to create their own breeds, such as the Chickasaw Indian Pony.

A famous herd of Mustangs lives in Nevada. They are known as Annie's Horses after Wild Horse Annie, who fought to protect feral horses and donkeys.

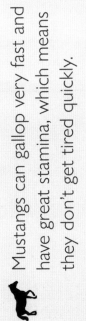 Mustangs can gallop very fast and have great stamina, which means they don't get tired quickly.

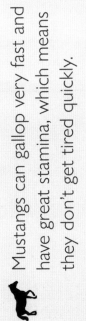 More than half of America's feral horses live in Nevada. A state coin shows three Mustangs on the back.

Fact file

Group: Light horse

Height: 14–15 hands (56–60 in; 142–152 cm)

Color: All colors

Character: Strong-willed

Comes from: Mexico and western United States

Used for: Lives wild

Andalusian

 The beautiful Andalusian horse has a long, arched neck and a flowing mane and tail.

 This horse is named after Andalusia in southern Spain. Its ancestors have lived in the region for thousands of years. Cave paintings of these ancient horses have been found going back more than twenty thousand years.

 Many of the first Andalusians were bred by Spanish monks, who kept detailed records of the horses they were breeding.

 In modern Spain the Andalusian is called *Pura Raza Española*, which means "pure Spanish breed."

 This tough, sturdy animal was once a popular warhorse in many different armies.

 Horses from Andalusia were once considered the best in the world. They were owned by the kings and aristocrats of Europe, and were expensive to buy.

Fact file

Group: Light horse

Height: 15–16 hands
(60–68 in; 152–173 cm)

Color: Mostly gray

Character: High-spirited

Comes from: Spain

Used for: Riding

Arab

 The Arab is thought to be descended from wild horses that once lived in the Arabian Desert. They were tamed by Bedouins, a group of nomads who wandered the desert.

 The Bedouins who first bred Arabs really loved their horses. They especially prized the mares. To stop them from being stolen, they let their horses stay with them in their tents at night.

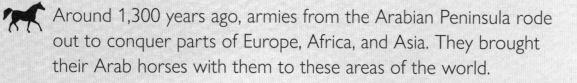 Around 1,300 years ago, armies from the Arabian Peninsula rode out to conquer parts of Europe, Africa, and Asia. They brought their Arab horses with them to these areas of the world.

 Because they come from the desert, Arab horses need less water and food than many other breeds. They can often outrun other breeds too.

Fact file

Group: Light horse

Height: Up to 15 hands (60 in; 152 cm)

Color: Bay, black, gray, chestnut, roan

Character: Sociable

Comes from: Arabian Peninsula

Used for: Riding

Arab horses did not become popular in Europe until people started racing horses The speedy Arab was used to breed English racehorses.

Knabstrupper

 The first Knabstruppers were bred around two hundred years ago in Denmark. The unusual markings of these beautiful horses made them one of the most popular breeds in Europe.

All Knabstruppers are descended from a mare called Flaebe. She was bought by Major Villars Lunn, who owned the Knabstrupgaard manor house on the Danish island of Zealand.

Like other spotted horses, the Knabstrupper has faint stripes on its hooves.

Fact file

Group: Light horse

Height: 14.2 hands or more
(58 in; 147 cm)

Color: Spotted

Character: Easy to train

Comes from: Denmark

Used for: Riding, pulling carriages

This Danish horse has long legs, which allow it to take big strides when it is galloping.

 The Knabstrupper is very intelligent and can be trained to perform in sports shows. Its wide back is perfect for gymnasts and athletes to ride on.

Basuto Pony

 Basuto Ponies come from Lesotho. This is a rugged, mountainous country in southern Africa.

 The sturdy, sure-footed Basuto is descended from the first horses to arrive in southern Africa. They were brought there by Dutch traders nearly 400 years ago.

The breed is named after the Basuto people of Lesotho. The kingdom of Lesotho used to be called Basutoland.

Today, Basuto Ponies carry tourists as they explore Lesotho's wild and beautiful landscape.

Basuto Ponies carried soldiers into battle and hauled food and equipment during the Boer Wars. These battles raged across South Africa around a hundred years ago.

The Basuto Pony has adapted to survive in its rugged home. It can withstand extreme hot and cold. Its hooves are very hard and help to protect its feet as it scrambles around the mountainous landscape.

Some of Lesotho's mountain roads are steep, full of holes and difficult to cross. The best way to get around remote areas is often on the back of a Basuto Pony.

Fact file

Group: Horse
Height: 14.2 hands (58 in; 147 cm)
Color: Chestnut, brown, gray, and bay
Character: Brave and docile
Comes from: Lesotho
Used for: Riding, pulling loads

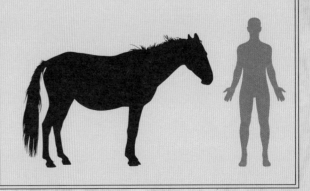

Icelandic Horse

🐴 The ancestors of the Icelandic Horse came to Iceland with their owners, who sailed all the way from Norway and Britain.

🐴 This breed is protected by law. No other horse breeds are allowed to mix with it. For 800 years, any Iceland Horse that left Iceland has not been allowed to come back.

🐴 Although it is only as big as a pony, the Icelandic Horse is strong for its size.

🐴 In winter, this sturdy survivor grows an extra-thick coat to help it cope with the freezing Icelandic weather. In spring, it sheds its winter coat.

🐴 Icelandic Horses come in many colors. This breed has up to forty different coat colors.

🐴 When Icelandic Horses have blue eyes, they are known as "glass" eyes. Some other breeds can have blue eyes too.

The Icelandic Horse can move in ways that many other breeds can't. It does a running walk called a tölt (pronounced "turlt") and a high-speed "flying pace."

Fact file

Group: Horse

Height: 12.1–14.1 hands (49–57 in; 124–145 cm)

Color: All colors

Character: Friendly

Comes from: Iceland

Used for: Riding

Falabella

 This little South American horse is the smallest horse breed in the world. It is no bigger than a large dog.

The Falabella's ancestors were small Spanish horses that lived on the Pampas, the grassy plains of South America.

The breed is named after Juan Falabella, who had a ranch in Argentina where these little horses were bred.

This miniature breed was created by mixing small Native American horses with Thoroughbreds, Criollos and Shetland Ponies.

Fact file

Group: Light horse

Height: 6.1–8.2 hands
   (25–34 in; 63–86 cm)

Color: All colors

Character: Calm

Comes from: Argentina

Used for: Pet, also riding,
   pulling carriages

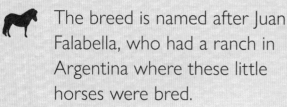

The Falabella was carefully bred as a miniature horse, with slender legs and a flowing mane and tail.

The little Falabella is not strong enough to carry a rider, except for a very small child. It can be used to pull a small carriage.

Most Falabellas now live in North America, where they are kept as pets.

Falabellas are intelligent and easy to train, so they are sometimes used as guide horses. Like guide dogs, they can help blind people to find their way around.

Shire

 This gentle English giant is one of the strongest horse breeds. A pair of Shire horses can pull 15 tons, which is much as seven big cars.

 The breed takes its name from the shires, or areas, of central England, such as Derbyshire, Lincolnshire, and Leicestershire. That is where most of England's Shire horses were once found.

 The Shire horse is famous for its feathering—the long, white hair that covers its sturdy lower legs.

 The Shire was once the workhorse of England. It did all the farmwork that tractors now do, pulling plows to dig the soil and harrows to smooth it.

 Once, breweries all over England used Shires to deliver their beer. Pairs of horses pulled carts loaded with beer barrels and delivered them to inns.

 A Shire called Perseus is owned by the queen of England. He is a drum horse, carrying a rider and two drums in royal ceremonies.

Fact file

Group: Heavy horse

Height: 16–17.2 hands
(64–70 in; 162–178 cm)

Color: Black, bay, gray, or roan

Character: Gentle

Comes from: Midlands, England

Used for: Riding, heavy work

Konik

The Konik pony comes from Poland. The word *konik* means "little horse" in Polish.

In remote areas of Poland, Konik ponies were once used for farmwork. When farmers couldn't afford to feed them over winter, the ponies were set free to graze in the wild. In spring, they were captured again.

This pony is small but strong too, so it is powerful enough to pull carts and plows.

In 1936, a reserve was opened for Koniks in the Bialowieza Forest in eastern Poland. This was once part of an ancient forest that stretched across Europe.

Herds of Koniks are used to help preserve natural grasslands and wetlands. By grazing on the plants there, the ponies stop trees and bushes taking over.

This breed is too small to carry adult riders, but Koniks are popular as a child's pony.

Fact file

Group: Pony

Height: up to 12.3–13.3 hands (51–55 in; 129–140 cm)

Color: Gray-brown

Character: Friendly, intelligent

Comes from: Poland

Used for: Lives semiwild, also used for light work and riding

Thoroughbred

 The Thoroughbred is the main breed used for racing. Once, any horses that could run fast were used in this way. Those early racehorses were known as running horses.

 A winning Thoroughbred can make millions in prize money for its owners, which makes it the most expensive horse breed of all. In 2006, a Thoroughbred called The Green Monkey was sold for $16 million.

The breed was created in England around three hundred years ago, when three Barb, Turkoman, and Arab stallions were crossed with English mares.

 Thoroughbreds are built for speed. They are lean and strong and have powerful back legs.

 The American Thoroughbred Seabiscuit did not look like a champion, but he became a legend of the racetrack. He had a film made about him called *Seabiscuit*.

To help improve other breeds, they are often crossed with Thoroughbreds.

Red Rum was one of the greatest English racehorses ever. This famous Thoroughbred won the Grand National race three times.

Fact file

Group: Light horse

Height: More than 15 hands (60 in; 152 cm)

Color: All solid colors

Character: Brave and high-spirited

Comes from: England

Used for: Riding, racing

Jutland

This heavy horse is named after a region called Jutland in Denmark.

Medieval knights liked to ride Jutlands in jousting tournaments, when they fought each other with lances.

Fact file

Group: Heavy horse

Height: 15–16.1 hands (60–65 in; 152–165 cm)

Color: Mostly chestnut

Character: Calm, good-natured

Comes from: Denmark

Used for: Pulling heavy loads, farmwork

In an old Danish story, a legendary hero called Svend rode a Jutland into battle with a giant. It was said to be the only breed of horse that was brave enough.

 Jutlands were once popular as warhorses.

 The Jutland is built for heavy work. Its strong, muscular body gives it all the power it needs to pull heavy wagons and carriages.

 This sturdy workhorse has been pulling plows and carts for hundreds of years. Today, Jutlands still haul beer wagons through Copenhagen, the capital of Denmark.

Brumby

 These hardy little horses roam free in Australia's wild, open spaces, or Outback. They live in large herds known as mobs or bands.

 The ancestors of the Brumby were used during the Australian Gold Rush, when thousands of people went looking for gold. The horses were let loose when the rush was over, around a hundred years ago.

 No one is sure how the Brumby got its name. It may come from *baroomby*, which means "wild" in the language of the Pitjara people, who have lived in Australia for thousands of years.

 Some farmers see Brumbies as pests because they eat crops and damage farm fences.

Brumbies can harm Australia's natural wildlife. They graze on wild plants and like to eat the same food as native animals, such as wallabies.

Thowra is a famous storybook Brumby. This stallion is the star of The Silver Brumby books, set in southeastern Australia.

Fact file

Group: Light horse

Height: 14–15 hands
(56–60 in; 142–152 cm)

Color: All colors

Character: Strong-willed

Comes from: Australia

Used for: Feral

Lipizzaner

 Lipizzaners are the stars of the Spanish Riding School in Vienna, Austria. People come from all over the world to watch these beautiful horses perform their dances accompanied by music.

 A Lipizzaner takes years to master all the movements it has to learn. These include amazing leaps and balancing on its back legs, which is called the levade and is incredibly difficult for a horse to do.

Only the best stallions are chosen for the Spanish Riding School. They are trained in the Winter Riding Hall, which was originally built as a riding school for boys from wealthy families.

Lipizzaners take their name from Lipizza, Slovenia, in Central Europe. This is where they were first bred. The village has now changed its name to Lipica.

Fact file

Group: Light horse

Height: 15–16 hands (60–64 in; 152–162 cm)

Color: Mostly gray

Character: Intelligent, willing

Comes from: Slovenia

Used for: Riding, pulling carriages

All the Lipizzaners alive today are descended from six stallions and 24 mares that were brought to Lipica from Spain more than four hundred years ago.

Newborn Lipizzaners are brown or black, but gradually turn gray as they get older.

The movements that Lipizzaners are taught were designed to help them defend their riders from attack.

Exmoor Pony

 Exmoor Ponies take their name from Exmoor, a hilly moorland region in southwest England where they once roamed semiwild.

 The Exmoor Pony is thought to have very ancient ancestors. It has lived on Exmoor for centuries, away from other horses.

 Horses similar to Exmoor Ponies were living in Britain 50,000 years ago.

Fact file

Group: Pony

Height: 11.2–12.3 hands (46–51 in; 117–130 cm)

Color: Bay, brown, dun

Character: Friendly

Comes from: England

Used for: Riding, pulling light loads

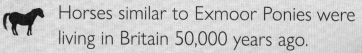

Ponies from Exmoor have been used as tame working animals since 400 BC. The Romans used them when they ruled Britain.

Farmers on the tough hill farms around Exmoor once relied completely on these ponies. They used them to herd sheep, plow fields, and take people to market.

Exmoors have "toad eyes", or extra-fleshy eyelids. They also have "snow chutes"—fans of bushy hair at the top of their tails. Both of these help to keep off the rain and snow on wet and windy Exmoor.

Exmoor Ponies help to protect moorland plants. They nibble neatly on coarser plants, leaving space for more delicate and rare ones to grow in between.

Friesian

 These beautiful horses are almost always glossy black, with no white markings.

 The breed comes from Friesland—a flat, open region of canals and farmland in the northern Netherlands.

 Friesian horses are strong for their size, and lift their knees high when trotting. They are used in trotting races to pull two-wheeled carts.

 The Friesian *sjees* (pronounced "shay-z") was a light carriage designed to be pulled by Friesian horses. It had two enormous wheels and could carry two people.

 Black Friesian horses are often used by undertakers to pull coffins in traditional, old-fashioned funerals.

 Friesians are gentle and easy to train, which makes them ideal for work in films. Friesian horses have starred in movies such as The Chronicles of Narnia and The Hunger Games series.

Fact file

Group: Light horse

Height: 15–16.3 hands
(60–67 in; 152–170 cm)

Color: Black

Character: Quick to learn

Comes from: The Netherlands

Used for: Riding, pulling carts

Brabant

 This huge horse is one of the heaviest and strongest of the heavy horses. It weighs twice as much as a racehorse and is also called the Belgian Draft.

 The powerful Brabant was specially bred to cope with the cold, wet weather and heavy soil on Belgian farms.

 Before the invention of tractors and trucks, this hardworking horse did all the heavy jobs on farms in Europe and America.

Horses similar to Brabants were used as warhorses in medieval times. Knights in full armor rode them into battle.

The Brabant was used in the breeding of the French Ardennais more than a hundred years ago. This large workhorse comes from northeastern Europe.

A Brabant called Brooklyn Supreme is probably the heaviest horse that has ever lived. He weighed 3,200lb (1,451kg), which is more than a small car.

Fact file

Group: Heavy horse

Height: 16.1–16.3 hands
(65–67 in; 165–170 cm)

Color: Bay, black, chestnut, roan,
sometimes gray

Character: Friendly

Comes from: Belgium

Used for: Pulling loads, farmwork

Tennessee Walking Horse

 This breed is famous for its "running walk", a super-fast way of walking.

 A Tennessee Walker may flap its ears and nod its head in time to each step in a running walk.

 The Narragansett Pacer was used to help develop the Tennessee Walker breed. The Pacer is the oldest American horse breed.

Fact file

Group: Light horse

Height: 14.3–17 hands
(59–68 in; 150–172 cm)

Color: All colors

Character: Calm

Comes from: United States

Used for: Riding

A famous stallion called Black Allan was one of the earliest Tennessee Walkers. He was born in 1886.

The Walker was bred for use on the plantations, or farms, in Tennessee. Plantation owners needed a horse that was comfortable to ride because they often had to spend all day in the saddle.

The Tennessee Walker moves in a smooth way that does not bounce its rider up and down.

Tennessee Walking Horses have been movie and TV stars. A Walker called Allen's Gold Zephyr played Trigger, the horse belonging to the famous cowboy Roy Rogers.

Quarter Horse

- This breed has huge muscles in its thighs. Over a short distance, it can outrun any other type of horse.

- The Quarter Horse is the oldest American breed. It was created by crossbreeding English and Spanish horses.

- Quarter horses got their name because of the quarter-mile races they used to run.

- More than a hundred years ago, cowboys working on ranches rode Quarter Horses to drive their cattle.

- This breed is said to have "cow sense" because it instinctively knows how to guide and herd cattle.

- The Quarter Horse is said to be the most popular breed in the world. Today, there are around 3 million Quarter Horses worldwide.

Quarter Horses can quickly put on speed and change direction. This makes them ideal for cowboys to ride in rodeos. In these competitions, the cowboys show off their skills.

Fact file

Group: Light horse

Height: 14.3–16 hands (59–64 in; 150–163 cm)

Color: Mainly reddish-brown, but can be other colors too

Character: Calm

Comes from: United States

Used for: Riding

Shetland Pony

- The Shetland Pony is one of the smallest breeds of horse.

- For its size, the Shetland Pony is one of the strongest horses in the world.

- Shetland Ponies were once transported across Britain to work in coal mines. They had to pull carts through small tunnels deep underground.

- These little ponies are named after the remote islands of Shetland off the north coast of Scotland, where they were first bred.

- Horses have lived on the Shetland islands for more than 2,500 years.

- Today's breed is thought to be descended from ponies that Vikings brought to the islands more than 1,000 years ago.

- Shetland has few trees and can be very wet and windy. The Pony's shaggy fur helps to keep it warm and dry.

- Today, Shetland Ponies are kept as pets in Britain and North America.

Fact file

Group: Pony
Height: 10.2 hands (42 in; 107 cm)
Color: All solid colors
Character: Independent, stubborn
Comes from: Shetland Islands
Used for: Riding, pulling carriages

Criollo

 Criollo horses live wild in South America, on the wide, open grasslands called the Pampas.

 The Criollo breed is said to be descended from just 100 Andalusian stallions that arrived in South America in 1535. The stallions sailed across the ocean all the way from Spain in the galleons of Spanish explorers.

The ancestors of the Criollo escaped from their Spanish owners. The horses ran off into the wild and began to breed.

The tough Criollo has adapted to survive the extreme heat and cold of its harsh Pampas home.

Fact file

Group: Light horse

Height: 13.3–14.3 hands
(55–59 in; 140–150 cm)

Color: Usually dun

Character: Easygoing

Comes from: South America

Used for: Riding, working
with cattle

Cowboys called gauchos round up cattle on the plains of South America. The horses they ride are bred from wild Criollos.

Criollos can travel long distances. In 1987, a Criollo called Sufridor was ridden all the way from South America to the Arctic. It took five and a half years.

Haflinger

The gentle, friendly Haflinger is a perfect horse for children and beginners to ride.

The first Haflingers were bred in the mountains of Austria and Italy. The breed takes its name from Hafling, in northeastern Italy.

All Haflingers are descended from a stallion called Folie, which was born in 1874 in a mountainous area called the Tyrol.

Haflingers were bred to survive in the rugged Alps, which are the highest mountains in Europe. These hardy little horses have strong hearts and lungs, which help them to cope with the thin mountain air.

High up in the Alps, Haflingers were once used to carry goods to remote villages and farms.

The Haflinger's coat is always golden-brown, with a blond mane and tail.

The Austrian and German armies still use Haflingers in steep, mountainous regions that motor vehicles and machinery cannot reach.

Around a hundred years ago, the Indian Army tried using Haflingers as packhorses in the hot, dry mountains of India. Their plan failed because the horses could not stand the heat.

Fact file

Group: Horse

Height: 13.2–14.3 hands
(54–59 in; 137–150 cm)

Color: Chestnut

Character: Friendly

Comes from: Austria

Used for: Riding, pulling loads

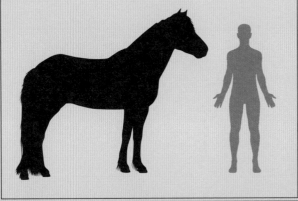

Appaloosa

 The Appaloosa comes from North America and is best known for its spotted coat.

 The ancestor of the Appaloosa is thought to be the Spanish horse, which European settlers brought with them to North America about 500 years ago.

 The Nez Perce people created the Appaloosa about 200 years ago. They let their horses roam free, but the animals' markings made it easier for their owners to recognize them.

 Appaloosas were first bred in the area around the Palouse River. They were known as Palouse horses, but gradually the name changed to Appaloosa.

 The Appaloosa's coat is covered with a pattern of spots and patches. These patterns vary. Each pattern has a different name, such as leopard-spotted, frosted hip, and snowflake.

Fact file

Group: Light horse
Height: 14 hands (56 in; 142 cm)
Color: Usually spotted
Character: Good-natured
Comes from: United States
Used for: Riding

An Appaloosa foal may not have a spotted coat when it is born, but its spots will begin to show as it gets older.

Most horses show the whites of their eyes only when they roll their eyes back. An Appaloosa shows the whites of its eyes at all times, just like humans.

Appaloosas often have striped hooves.

Welsh Cob

The Welsh Cob is the largest of the Welsh Ponies. Ponies have roamed the moors and mountains of Wales for thousands of years.

A cob is a small, sturdy horse with strong limbs. Cobs are calm and steady animals.

British knights are thought to have ridden Welsh Cobs into battle. The Cobs had to lead the heavier warhorses, and had to keep up to speed with their bigger and faster companions.

The British Army once used Welsh Cobs to pull heavy guns and equipment. The horses could travel over land that motor vehicles could not cross.

Fact file

Group: Light horse

Height: More than 13.2 hands (54 in; 137 cm)

Color: All solid colors

Character: Friendly

Comes from: Wales

Used for: Riding, pulling loads

Before cars, the best way to get around Wales was with a Welsh Cob. A pony had to prove its strength by doing an uphill journey of 35 miles (56 km) in under three hours.

Until the 1960s, the Welsh Cob and other Welsh Ponies were used by cart drivers to deliver milk and food.

Percheron

 This big, strong breed is named after Le Perche, an ancient region in northern France.

 The ancestors of the Percheron are probably the warhorses of the Moors from North Africa. These invaders tried to conquer France about 1,300 years ago, and left their horses behind.

 This mighty workhorse was created mostly by crossbreeding Arab stallions with mares from France and Belgium.

 A stallion called Jean le Blanc was the first Percheron. His name means "John the White," and he was born in 1823.

Fact file

Group: Heavy horse

Height: 16.1–16.2 hands or more (65–66 in; 165–167 cm)

Color: Mostly gray and black

Character: Calm, good-natured

Comes from: Northern France

Used for: Hauling carts, coaches, and plows

Unlike some other heavy horses, the Percheron does not have feathering, or long, fluffy hair, on its lower legs. This helps to keep its legs clean when it is working in muddy fields.

A Percheron called Dr. LeGear was famous for his huge size. He lived in Missouri about a hundred years ago.

Marwari

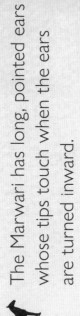

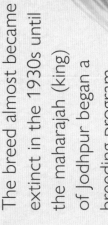

- This breed is named after Marwar, a dry, desert region in western India. The old Kingdom of Mawar was also known as Jodhpur, which gives its name to jodhpurs, the specially shaped trousers that riders once wore.

- The trustworthy Marwari was legendary for always being able to find its way home, even from far away. It always carried its rider to safety, despite being injured itself.

- The Indian cavalry—the soldiers who ride on horseback—always used Marwari horses.

- Like many other horses, Marwaris have excellent hearing and can pick up sounds from far away. They can warn their riders of danger ahead.

- The Marwari has long, pointed ears whose tips touch when the ears are turned inward.

- The breed almost became extinct in the 1930s until the maharajah (king) of Jodhpur began a breeding program.

Purebred Marwaris are very rare today. The Indian government keeps a record of the breed to make that sure it survives.

Fact file

Group: Light horse

Height: 15 hands (60 in; 152 cm)

Color: All colors

Character: Good-tempered

Comes from: India

Used for: Riding, pulling carriages

Don

🐎 The Don is descended from semiwild horses that lived on the vast, treeless grasslands in Russia called the steppes.

🐎 The first Don horses were bred around two hundred years ago in the region around the river Don in Russia.

🐎 Dons are not as easy to ride as many other breeds of horse. They have upright shoulders, which makes them bounce up and down as they walk and run.

🐎 The Don was bred to be tough and hard-working. It had to be able to keep going even when there was not much food around.

🐎 Fierce Russian warriors called Cossacks were the first people to ride these brave and swift horses. The Cossacks were highly skilled horsemen.

🐎 Just over two hundred years ago, a mighty French army invaded Russia. Thousands of Cossacks riding Don horses helped to defeat the French.

Fact file

Group: Light horse

Height: 15.2–16.2 hands
(62–66 in; 157–167 cm)

Color: Mostly chestnut

Character: Good-natured

Comes from: Russia

Used for: Riding, pulling carriages

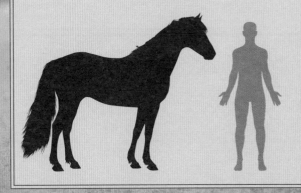

Australian Stock Horse

 The Stock Horse is strong, fast and fit. It is ideal for work on the vast cattle and sheep ranches in the Australian Outback.

This workhorse is one of the world's newest breeds. The first Stock Horses were bred just sixty years ago.

Fact file

Group: Light horse

Height: 14.2–16 hands
(58–64 in; 147–162 cm)

Color: All solid colors

Character: Intelligent

Comes from: Australia

Used for: Riding, working with cattle

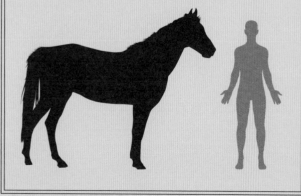

The Australian Stock Horse is descended from the Waler. This was a type of horse that was named after the state of New South Wales in southeastern Australia.

Although it was bred for use on cattle ranches, the Australian Stock Horse is good at other activities too. It performs in horse shows and is used in the sport of polo.

The Stock Horse is popular for campdrafting. In this Australian sport, a horse and rider guide a cow through a twisting course.

Today, Australian ranchers often use motorbikes or helicopters instead of horses to round up their cattle. But Stock Horses are still used in the rugged, mountainous areas that vehicles cannot reach.

Orlov Trotter

 The Orlov Trotter is named after Count Alexei Orlov, the Russian nobleman who created the breed around two hundred years ago.

 Count Orlov wanted a horse that was fast, strong and calm, so he crossed Arab stallions with mares from Spain, England, the Netherlands, and Denmark.

 An Arab stallion called Smetanka was the ancestor of all Trotters. He was given to Count Orlov after he won an important battle against the Turkish navy.

 The Orlov Trotter has a long, straight body and pulls carriages quickly and smoothly.

Fact file

Group: Light horse

Height: 15.1–17 hands
(61–68 in; 155–173 cm)

Color: Gray, bay, black, chestnut

Character: Calm, friendly

Comes from: Russia

Used for: Pulling carriages, riding, racing

The breed is called a trotter because it can trot at high speed and can be used for racing.

Trottors are still used in carriage races across Russia. Three horses joined together by a troika harness run side by side across the snow, with their bells jingling.

American Paint Horse

 The American Paint Horse gets its name from the large splashes of color on its coat. It looks as if someone has daubed it with paint.

Paint Horses have three different coat patterns. Tobiano is white with patches of color, while overo has a colored background with white areas. Tovero is a mixture of the two.

The Paint Horse is said to be descended from Spanish horses that escaped into the wild. They roamed the plains and deserts of the American West.

Fact file

Group: Light horse

Height: 15–16 hands
(60–64 in; 152–163 cm)

Color: Any color

Character: Easygoing

Comes from: United States

Used for: Riding

Native Americans have a special name for a Paint Horse with a dark patch over its ears and head. They say it has a "medicine hat", and believe that it will protect them and bring good luck.

The Paint Horse can gallop really fast. Cowboys and cattle ranchers use this breed because they need swift horses for rounding up cattle.

Today, American Paint Horses are mostly found in Texas and on the warm, dry prairies of the United States.

Fjord

 This tough little breed is thought to be related to ancient wild horses from Asia and Europe. Its ancestors made their way to Norway and were tamed by the people there more than 4,000 years ago.

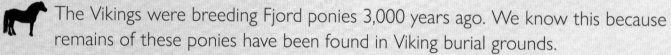

Fjords are long inlets with steep sides along the coast of Norway. The Fjord pony is strong and sure-footed enough to plow the sloping fields around these fjords.

The Vikings were breeding Fjord ponies 3,000 years ago. We know this because remains of these ponies have been found in Viking burial grounds.

In Norway, ancient stone carvings show fighting stallions that look just like Fjord ponies.

Viking adventurers took Fjord ponies with them across the sea to Iceland, Britain, and Ireland. They used them as warhorses.

Fact file

Group: Pony

Height: 13–14.2 hands
  (52–58 in; 132–147 cm)

Color: Pale brown

Character: Mellow

Comes from: Norway

Used for: Riding, pulling carts

The breed has a thick coat to keep it warm in the freezing Norwegian winter. Its mane is usually trimmed so that it stands up, like a ridge of bristles, along its neck.

All Fjord ponies are dun in color, which is a type of pale brown. They also have a dark stripe along their backs.

This breed has very small ears compared to other horses. Bigger ears would freeze and be easily injured in the cold Norwegian winters.

Noriker

 The first Norikers are thought to have come from the area around the Grossglockner, the highest mountain in Austria.

 The Noriker's ancestors were large Roman warhorses. The Romans brought them to the Austrian Alps more than two thousand years ago.

 This heavy breed takes its name from Noricum, which was the Roman word for Austria.

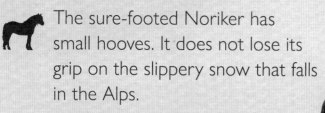 The sure-footed Noriker has small hooves. It does not lose its grip on the slippery snow that falls in the Alps.

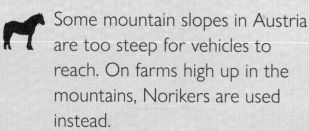 Some mountain slopes in Austria are too steep for vehicles to reach. On farms high up in the mountains, Norikers are used instead.

 The Noriker has a huge neck and a wide, round body. This shape is ideal for hauling wagons.

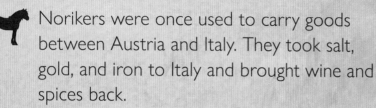 Norikers were once used to carry goods between Austria and Italy. They took salt, gold, and iron to Italy and brought wine and spices back.

A contest called the Kufenstechen is held every year in southern Austria. Young men riding bareback on Noriker horses have to smash a wooden barrel with an iron club.

Fact file

Group: Heavy horse

Height: 15.1–16.3 hands (61–67 in; 155–170 cm)

Color: Black, bay, chestnut, roan with spotted coats

Character: Friendly

Comes from: Austria

Used for: Pulling wagons

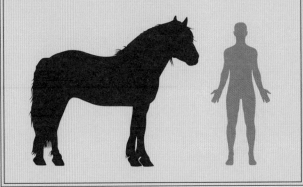

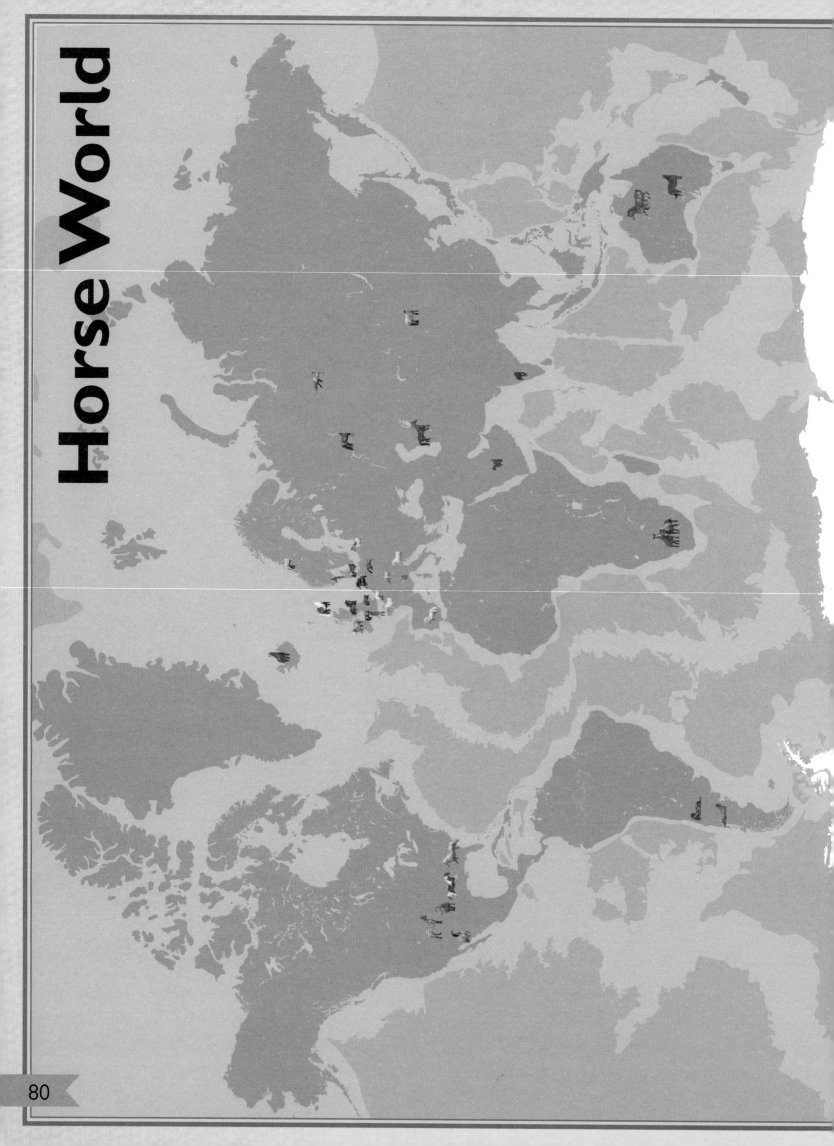